Flute
Grade 2

Pieces
for Trinity College London exams

2017-2022

Published by
Trinity College London Press Ltd
trinitycollege.com

Registered in England
Company no. 09726123

Copyright © 2016 Trinity College London Press Ltd
Third impression, June 2021

Unauthorised photocopying is illegal
No part of this publication may be copied or reproduced in any
form or by any means without the prior permission of the publisher.

Printed in England by Halstan & Co, Amersham, Bucks

Group A

Touchstone

Louise Chamberlain
(b. 1947)

Copyright © 2003 by Faber Music Ltd. All rights reserved.

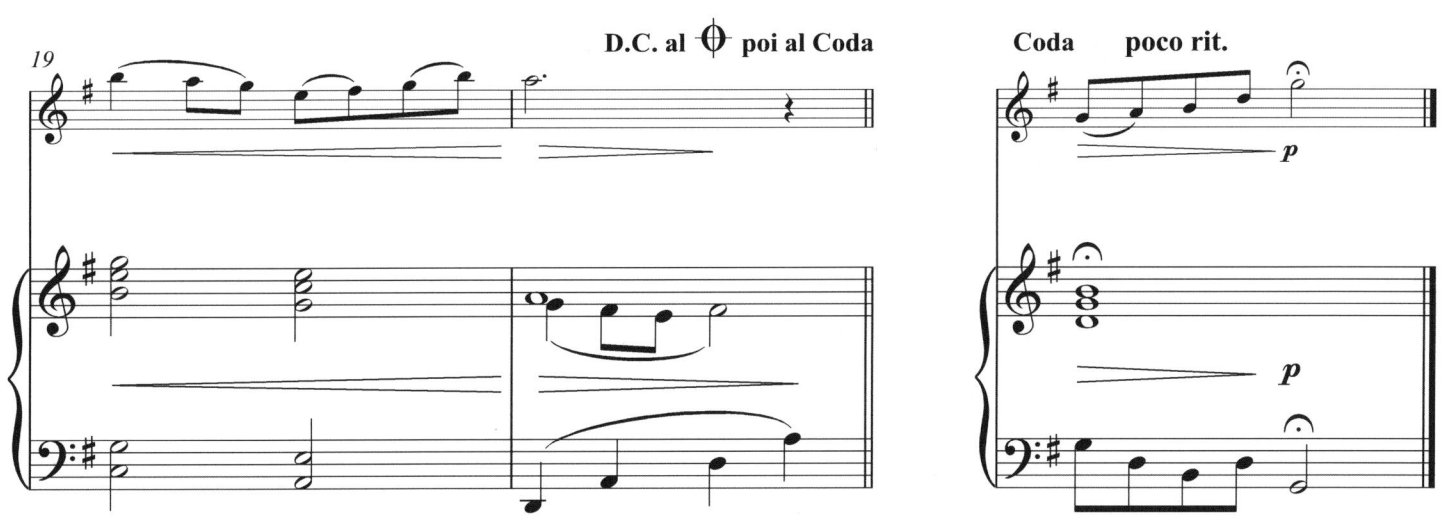

Group A

Riffs

Alan Haughton
(b. 1950)

Group A

The Sailor's Dance
from *Dido and Aeneas*

Henry Purcell
(1659–1695)

Group A

The Dance of the Snow Queen

Nikki Iles
(b. 1963)

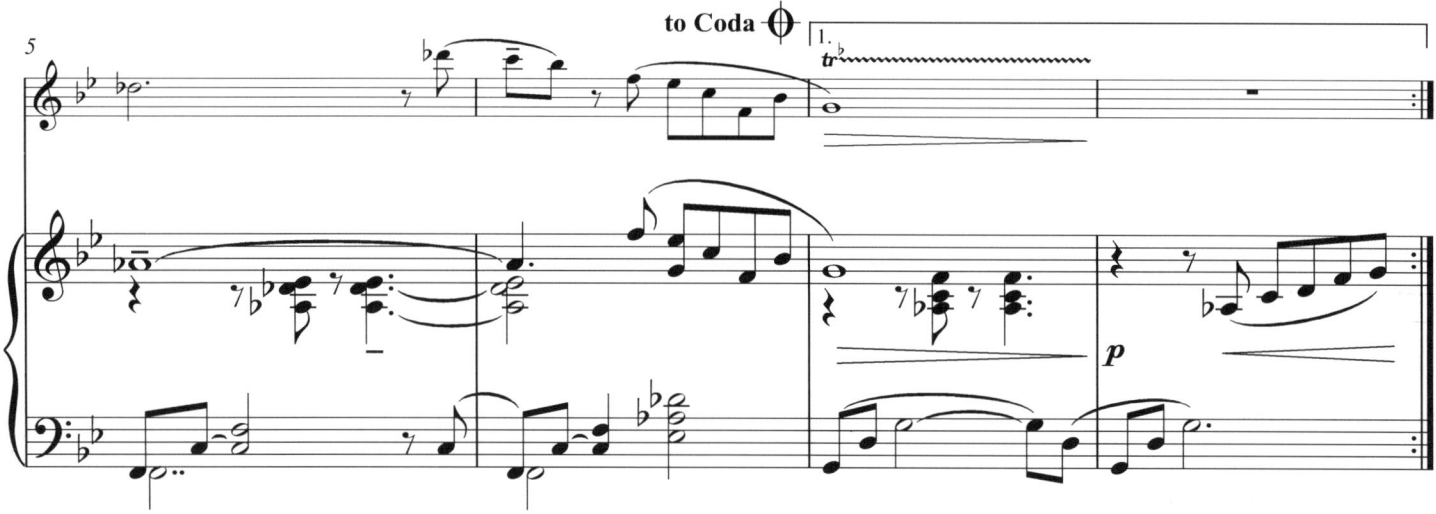

Copyright © 2006 by Faber Music Ltd. All rights reserved.

Group A

Paint It Black

Arr. Paul Hart

Mick Jagger (b. 1943)
and Keith Richards (b. 1943)

Copyright © 1966 Abco Music Inc. from *Hartbeat for Flute*
arr. Paul Hart published Brass Wind Publications; www.brasswindpublications.co.uk
Used by permission. All rights reserved. International copyright secured.

Group A

When the Boat Comes In
(*Dance ti' thy Daddy*)

Arr. Hywel Davies

Traditional

Copyright © 2013 by Boosey & Hawkes Music Publishers Ltd.
Reproduced by permission of Boosey & Hawkes Music Publishers Ltd.

Flute
Grade 2

Pieces
for Trinity College London exams

2017-2022

Published by
Trinity College London Press Ltd
trinitycollege.com

Registered in England
Company no. 09726123

Copyright © 2016 Trinity College London Press Ltd
Third impression, June 2021

Unauthorised photocopying is illegal
No part of this publication may be copied or reproduced in any
form or by any means without the prior permission of the publisher.

Printed in England by Halstan & Co, Amersham, Bucks

TCL 015518
ISBN 978-0-85736-506-4

Group A

Touchstone

Louise Chamberlain
(b. 1947)

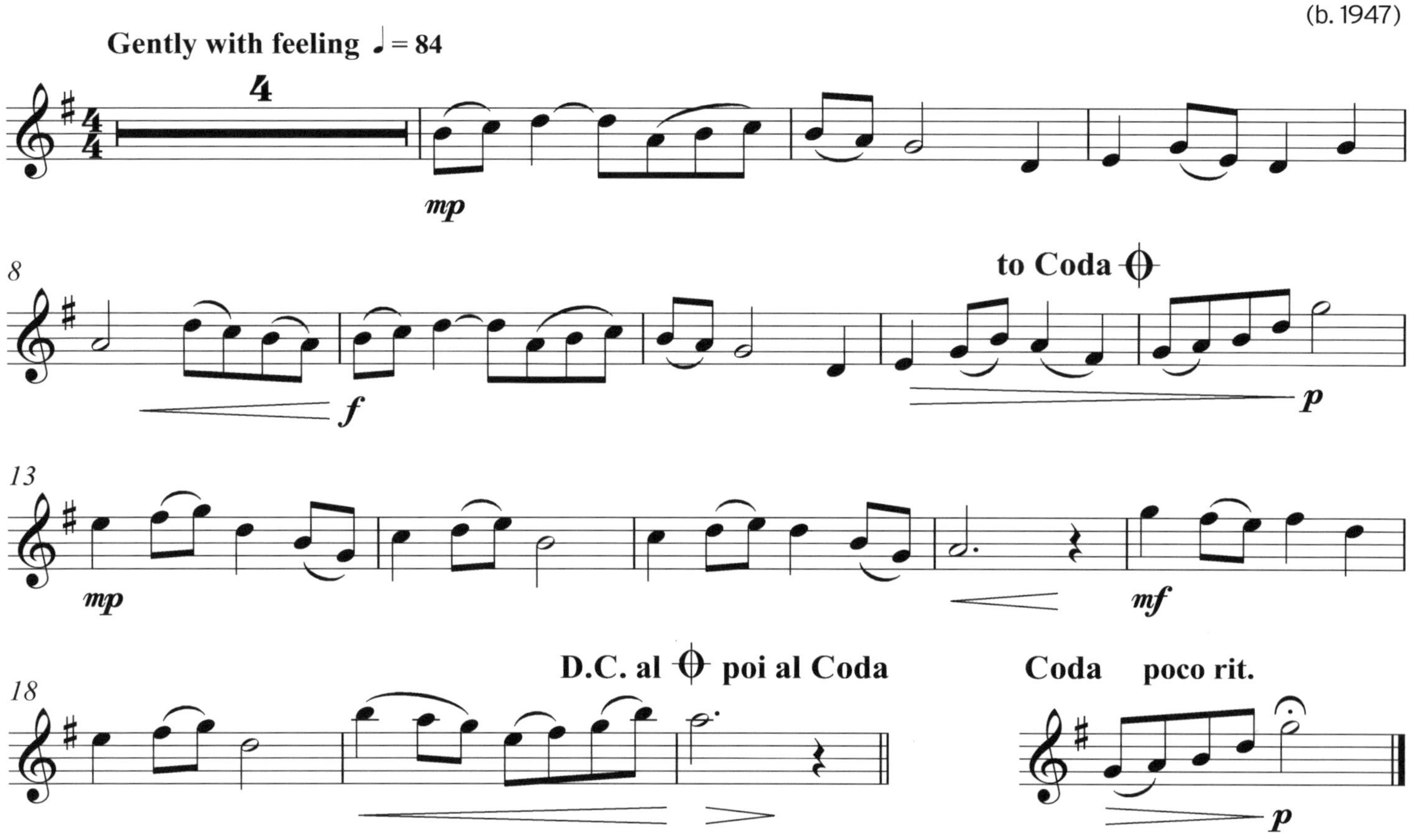

Copyright © 2003 by Faber Music Ltd. All rights reserved.

Riffs

Group A

The Sailor's Dance

from *Dido and Aeneas*

Henry Purcell
(1659–1695)

Copyright © 2014 Schott Music Ltd, London.
Reproduced by permission. All rights reserved.

Group A

The Dance of the Snow Queen

Nikki Iles
(b. 1963)

Group A

Paint It Black

Arr. Paul Hart

Mick Jagger (b. 1943)
and Keith Richards (b. 1943)

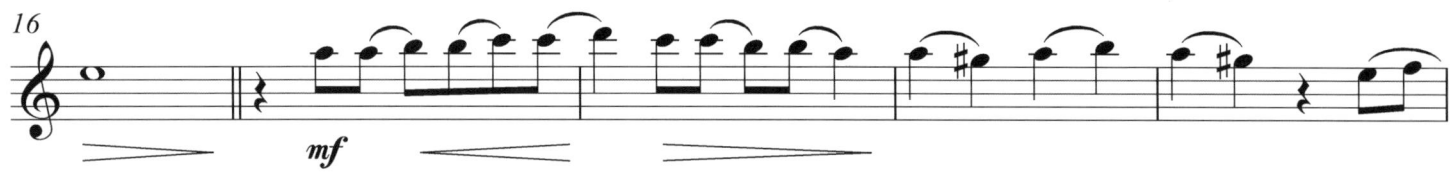

Copyright © 1966 Abco Music Inc. from *Hartbeat for Flute*
arr. Paul Hart published Brass Wind Publications; www.brasswindpublications.co.uk
Used by permission. All rights reserved. International copyright secured.

Group A

When the Boat Comes In
(Dance ti' thy Daddy)

Arr. Hywel Davies

Traditional

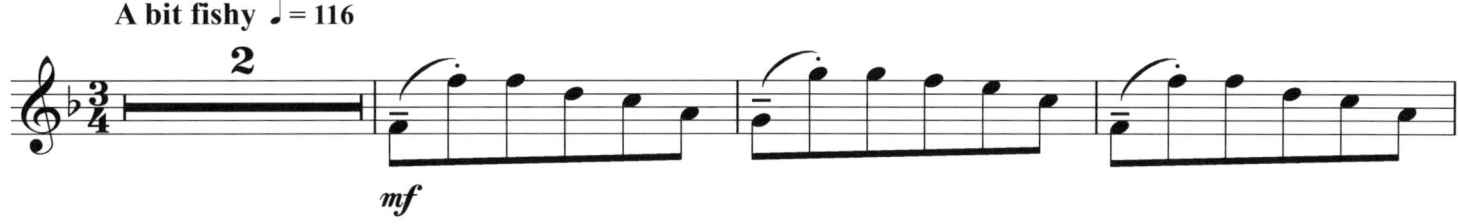

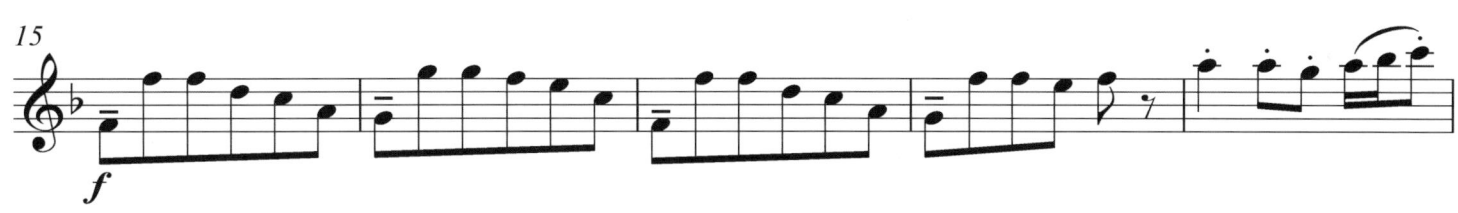

Copyright © 2013 by Boosey & Hawkes Music Publishers Ltd.
Reproduced by permission of Boosey & Hawkes Music Publishers Ltd.

Group B

Air Hollandais

Jules Demersseman
(b. 1833-1866)

Maestoso [♩ = 105]

Copyright © 2016 Trinity College London Press

Bouncin'

Ian Green

Bouncy [♩. = 90]

Copyright © 2003 by Boosey & Hawkes Music Publishers Ltd.
Reproduced by permission of Boosey & Hawkes Music Publishers Ltd.

Group B

You Said

Oliver Ledbury